"Charting New Waters: Adam and Emily's Journey to the Sea Life Center"

AF484706

Journey to the Sea Life Centre

The Impact Chronicles, Volume 6

Paul Smith

Published by Paul Smith, 2024.

While every precaution has been taken in the preparation of this book, the publisher assumes no responsibility for errors or omissions, or for damages resulting from the use of the information contained herein.

JOURNEY TO THE SEA LIFE CENTRE

First edition. March 1, 2024.

Copyright © 2024 Paul Smith.

ISBN: 979-8224896967

Written by Paul Smith.

Table of Contents

Chapter 1: A Fresh Start 1

Chapter 2: The Vision Takes Shape 3

Chapter 3: A Stroke of Luck 5

Chapter 4: Rallying Support 7

Chapter 5: Facing Challenges 9

Chapter 6: A Beacon of Hope 11

Chapter 7: The Grand Opening.................................... 15

Chapter 8: Navigating Challenges 17

Chapter 9: Making Connections 19

Chapter 10: Looking Ahead 21

Chapter 11: Weathering the Winter 23

Chapter 12: Springtime Surprises 25

Chapter 13: Welcoming Back the Wonders of the Sea.................. 27

Chapter 14: Embracing the Journey............................. 29

Chapter 15: Answering the Call................................... 31

Chapter 16: A Triumph on the Shore 33

Chapter 17: Sharing Stories.. 35

Chapter 18: The Spotlight.. 37

Chapter 19: Facing New Challenges 41

Chapter 20: A Promise Renewed................................. 43

"Charting New Waters" follows the inspiring journey of Adam and Emilys as they embark on a new endeavour to establish a sea and fish life sanctuary centre in the coastal town of Ramsey. Driven by their passion for marine conservation and mental health awareness, Adam and Emily navigate the challenges of securing funding and transforming an old building into a sanctuary centre, they face both triumphs and setbacks. From rallying community support to overcoming financial struggles, the couple demonstrates unwavering determination and resilience in the face of adversity.

Introduction: Before Sealife and the Rising Tide

As Adam and Emily embark on this new endeavor together, they can lean on each other for support and strength, further highlighting the importance of meaningful connections and relationships in overcoming challenges.

Overall, weaving together personal struggles, motivations, and a commitment to making a difference creates a rich and impactful story.

Adam's passion and determination despite financial constraints and scepticism from the town added layers of tension and conflict to their story, making his journey even more difficult as they could not believe how hard it was to secure funds or investors at a time of uncertainty. His unwavering belief in the importance of mental health awareness and suicide prevention drives him to find creative solutions with his fish tank worlds and rallys support from unlikely sources to showcase his fish tanks when and wherever possible picking up multiple connection and nominations in the industry.

Perhaps Adam's persistence in the face of adversity inspires others in the community to rally behind the cause, demonstrating the power of collective action and community support. Despite the challenges, Adam's vision and commitment ignite a sense of hope and purpose in those around him as his passion is clearly there just not enough funds, so thats why he started writing everything down hoping one day it transpired into a story of hope.

Additionally, the financial struggles and scepticism from the town shows their ability to navigate these challenges together and this only strengthens their bond and reinforces the message of perseverance in the face of adversity.

As they work tirelessly to bring "Sealife" to fruition, Adam and Emily's journey becomes not only a story of personal growth and redemption but also a testament to the transformative power of compassion and determination.

As the story unfolds, the success of the fundraising campaign and the transformation of the space can serve as milestones that highlight the impact of Adam and Emily's efforts, fueling their determination to continue making a positive difference in the lives of others.

The community coming together to volunteer their time and skills to transform the gallery into an accessible and welcoming space is a heartwarming addition to their story. Their willingness to pitch in highlights the strong sense of solidarity and shared purpose within the community.

Join Adam and Emily as they face many obstacles and changes that confront their dreams.

"Charting New Waters: Adam and Emily's Journey to the Sea Life Sanctuary Center":

In "Charting New Waters," marine biologists Adam and Emily embark on a daring quest to establish the Sea and Tropical Life Sanctuary Center in their coastal town of Ramsey. Faced with change, they see an opportunity to rebuild and revitalise their community by creating a sanctuary that celebrates and preserves marine life.

Driven by their passion for the ocean and a desire to make a positive impact, Adam and Emily set out to find the perfect location for their sanctuary centre. Along the way, they encounter numerous challenges, from sceptical town officials to financial obstacles. Undeterred, they rally support from the community, organising fundraising events and outreach efforts to garner resources and build momentum for their cause.

As they navigate the highs and lows of their journey, Adam and Emily's bond grows stronger, fueled by their shared vision and determination. Together, they overcome obstacles and setbacks, drawing inspiration from the beauty and resilience of the ocean they seek to protect.

With perseverance and tenacity, Adam and Emily finally secure the necessary funds and acquire the ideal building for their sanctuary centre. As they celebrate their victory with the community, they look ahead to a future filled with promise and possibility, where the Sea Life Sanctuary Center stands as a beacon of hope and renewal for generations to come.

"Charting New Waters" is a heartwarming tale of courage, community, and the power of one couple's dream to make a difference in the world. It reminds us that even in the face of adversity, the human spirit can prevail, and together, we can chart new waters and create a brighter future for all.

Chapter 1 of "Charting New Waters: Adam and Emily's Journey to the Sea Life Sanctuary Center":

Chapter 1: A Fresh Start

The morning sun cast a golden glow over the quaint coastal town of Ramsey as Adam and Emily stepped out of their modest shop, Ocean's Edge, onto the bustling street. The salty breeze carried the promise of a new day, and with it, the anticipation of new beginnings.

Adam adjusted his glasses and glanced up at the weathered sign that hung above the entrance, its faded letters spelling out the name of their shop in peeling paint. Ocean's Edge had been their labour of love for the past few years, a humble space where they shared their passion for marine life with the community through educational exhibits and handcrafted souvenirs.

As they locked the door behind them, Emily turned to Adam with a hopeful smile. "I have a good feeling about today," she said, her eyes sparkling with excitement.

Adam returned her smile, feeling a surge of optimism course through him. "Me too," he replied, his voice tinged with determination. "I think it's time we set our sights on something bigger."

With that, they set off down the cobblestone street, their footsteps echoing against the facades of colourful storefronts and quaint cottages. The town was buzzing with activity, the air alive with the sound of seagulls crying overhead and the chatter of locals going about their day.

As they walked, Adam and Emily discussed their dreams for the future, their voices filled with enthusiasm and possibility. They spoke of creating a sanctuary for marine life, a place where people could come to learn, explore, and connect with the ocean in new and meaningful ways.

Their conversation was interrupted by the sound of church bells ringing in the distance, signalling the start of a new day. Adam and Emily exchanged a glance, their resolve strengthened by the promise of what lay ahead.

"Let's make today the beginning of something extraordinary," Emily said, her voice ringing with conviction.

Adam nodded, his gaze fixed on the horizon where the sea met the sky. "Let's chart new waters," he said, his heart brimming with hope.

Together, they forged ahead, ready to embark on the journey of a lifetime.

Chapter 2: The Vision Takes Shape

With their hearts set on a new endeavour, Adam and Emily wasted no time in laying the groundwork for their vision. They spent countless hours poring over maps, researching potential locations, and brainstorming ideas for their sea and tank life sanctuary centre.

Their shop, Ocean's Edge, had served them well, but they knew it was time to dream bigger. They envisioned a space where people could come to learn about marine life, experience the wonders of the ocean firsthand, and be inspired to take action to protect it.

As they delved deeper into their plans, they found themselves drawn to the idea of repurposing an existing building in the heart of town. They imagined transforming it into a vibrant hub of activity, with exhibits, interactive displays, and a cafe where visitors could relax and soak in the breathtaking views of the harbour.

With their vision taking shape, Adam and Emily set out to find the perfect location for their sanctuary centre. They scoured the town, exploring every nook and cranny in search of the ideal space that would serve as the foundation for their dreams.

Chapter 3: A Stroke of Luck

After weeks of searching, Adam and Emily's perseverance paid off when they stumbled upon an old building tucked away on a quiet street near the waterfront. The building was a relic from the past, its faded facade bearing the marks of time and neglect.

But as Adam and Emily stepped inside, they felt a sense of possibility wash over them. The building had character and charm, with its high ceilings, large windows, and spacious layout. It was the perfect canvas for their vision, a blank slate waiting to be transformed into something extraordinary.

Excitement bubbled up inside them as they explored every corner of the building, imagining how it could be brought to life as their sanctuary centre, envisioning a wall of tanks over there and tall jelly fish tanks on this side where people walk in. They also envisioned exhibits showcasing the diversity of marine life as they guided guests round the different tanks of wonder. They would have interactive tanks on the bottom floor where visitors could get up close and personal with sea creatures, whilst learning about their habitats. The second floor opened up to be a spacious study room large enough to host the classes and exhibit local artist work amongst the world of planted tanks. The top floor amazed both Adam and Emily with its panoramic views of the harbour and mountain. They knew they found something special, something that would grow with them both. They knew as they left the agent smiling they had found it a newfound sense of purpose.

Adam and Emily set to work immediately, determined to turn their vision into reality.

Chapter 4: Rallying Support

As word spread of Adam and Emily's plans for the old building, the community loved the ideas too, so they rallied behind them with overwhelming support. Friends, neighbours, and local businesses offered their assistance, eager to lend a hand in any way they could.

Volunteers came forward to help with renovations, donations poured in to fund the project, and local artists offered to contribute their talents to create murals and sculptures for the sanctuary centre. The outpouring of generosity and goodwill filled Adam and Emily's hearts with gratitude, reinforcing their belief in the power of community.

With the support of their friends and neighbours, Adam and Emily forged ahead, working tirelessly to bring their vision to life. They had help from local electricians with fixing the wiring and the lift access was fully working again. The plumbers worked tirelessly as they fitted the tanks into position. The lighting and painting was almost complete.

Chapter 5: Facing Challenges

But as they delved deeper into the renovation process, Adam and Emily encountered unexpected challenges that threatened to derail their plans. The building was in worse condition than they had initially realised, with structural issues upstairs, water damage, and outdated utilities that needed to be addressed, the list was growing.

Faced with mounting expenses and setbacks, Adam and Emily found themselves grappling with doubt and uncertainty. But they refused to give up hope, drawing strength from their shared determination and experiences to see their vision through to the end they asked for help.

With the support of their community friends behind them providing them with solutions like donations from local trades people, Adam and Emily pressed on, tackling each challenge with grit and determination by picking up the phone and asking for help with the building and other ways to approach it. They knew that the road ahead would be difficult, but they also knew that the reward would be so worth it in the end as they could see the gallery taking shape although not a sign of a fish anywhere. With new toilets and promises of solar and green solutions to help with energy bills the gallery was alive with expectations.

Chapter 6: A Beacon of Hope

As the renovation work progressed, Adam and Emily's sanctuary and rescue centre began to take shape just as Adam envisaged, with the walled tanks and huge centre pool it was now an ocean inside. As you walk into the Sealife room your senses are overwhelmed with the smells, heat, and moistures like you have just landed at one of tropical zoos in the far east. This sea world transports you along different parts of the planet and showcases all the different fish species you would encounter on your travels. This magical tour transports you around the world and back to the murky waters of the Irish sea.

Once you're back, you might be needing a refreshment from all the excitement. Then guests can either visit the relaxing planted room of tropical fish tanks and reptiles or relax in the Aires Cafe' on the top floor overlooking the harbour and mountain views with light refreshments.

The Fish Box has emerged from the rubble as a beacon of hope and possibility for the town of Ramsey. The once-soulless empty building was now transformed into a vibrant and bustling space, alive with life and the energy of creativity and innovation.

Exhibits showcasing the wonders of marine life filled the spaces, with the tanks starting to be filled with the aquadecor and plants it wouldn't be long before they were teeming with colourful fish, coral reefs, and exotic sea creatures. The new delivery of the Interactive displays gave great hope as these invited visitors to learn about ocean creatures and conservation efforts, and encouraged them to take action to protect the environment. The equipment that was being delivered was out of this world and the couple could not be more thankful as more boxes turned up.

Emily was busy on the top floor, overlooking the harbour, the eating and lounging areas were now taking place, however Adam promised more tanks upstairs but he's too busy with his ones at the moment. The Cafe is starting to take shape but was a long way from their completed vision but the tiny kitchen is now fitted. This idea of a cafe like it used to be 60 years ago has excited the locals and has quickly become a favourite topic amongst them so they want to get the Cafe right. They were independent traders after all and they want customers to feel relaxed and enriched with knowledge and peace as they take in the natural beauty of their position.

They envisioned the Cafe one way during the day and another way during the night, a gathering spot for fish enthusiasts and tourists alike, its cosy atmosphere and stunning views drawing people in from far and wide across the island.

Overall, the community-driven new transformation of the gallery and its utilities. The Aires Cafe' not only serves a practical purpose but also symbolises the power of community collaboration and connection and a place to create positive changes.

It was always Emily's passion to have an evening dining room where it's intimate for the guests to experience a romantic evening overlooking the lit bay and tranquil mood lighting from the fish tanks was a perfect match.

Emily's vision for an intimate evening dining room perfectly complements the overall ambiance of the gallery and the Aires Cafe'. Her desire to create a romantic atmosphere overlooking the bay, with the gentle glow of mood lighting from the fish tanks, adds a touch of elegance and sophistication to the space.

The evening dining room not only serves as a revenue-generating opportunity for the charity but also enhances the overall visitor experience, providing a unique and memorable setting for special occasions and romantic evenings. The combination of stunning views, tranquil surroundings, and exquisite cuisine creates an atmosphere of warmth and intimacy that resonates with the island guests.

Emily's passion for creating memorable dining experiences aligns seamlessly with the charity's mission of promoting mental health awareness and well-being. Through the evening dining room, she not only contributes to the sustainability of the charity but also fosters connections and moments of joy for guests, furthering the importance of the charity's impact on the community.

By revitalising the cafe shop, Adam and Emily not only breathed new life into the building but also created a welcoming space for visitors to relax, socialise, and enjoy the stunning views of the harbour and surrounding area. It became a focal point of the SeaLife Sanctuary Center, enhancing the overall visitor experience and contributing to the centre's success.

As Adam and Emily worked together to bring their respective visions to life, their strengthened partnership has deepened their commitment to making a positive difference in the lives of others in the town. Now the exhibition tanks with their mood lighting have been installed by Adam. The evening dining room transforms into a spectacle of lights, sights and smells that excites the senses. The dining room becomes not only a symbol of their shared passion and dedication but also a testament to the transformative power of love and compassion as time allows things to grow.

On the eve of the big day, Adam and Emily stood hand in hand outside the newly renovated building, gazing up at its transformed facade with a mixture of pride and awe. It was hard to believe how far they had come since that fateful day when they first set foot inside the old building.

With its doors finally getting ready to be opened to the public tomorrow, there was a great sense of pride and achievement around everywhere and everyone involved was so upbeat. Adam and Emily took a moment outside again and stood back, looking at everything they had created in these short months and Adam Thanked Emily for this dream of dreams she had shared with him. He loved her more than anything physical as he knew he had sent his guardian angel to look after him and join this epic adventure. He was so excited as more fish deliveries would be coming soon and later that week.

Adam and Emily's Sea Life Sanctuary became a symbol of hope and renewal for the town of Ramsey, a testament to the power of vision, perseverance, and the community was excited to see the new results.

Chapter 7: The Grand Opening

As the final touches were nearly done and the new fish put in place, anticipation built for the grand opening of Adam and Emily's sea life sanctuary centre. Excitement rippled through the town of Ramsey, and anticipation hung in the air like a tangible presence.

The community had come together in remarkable ways to support their endeavour, and Adam and Emily were filled with gratitude for the generosity and kindness they had encountered along the way. They knew that the success of their sanctuary centre was thanks in large part to the unwavering support of their friends, neighbours, and fellow citizens of Ramsey.

As dawn broke on the day of the grand opening, it was bright and chilly in the fresh air. There was a sense of excitement as people woke up. The streets were soon alive with activity as people made their way out that day to see the new sanctuary centre, eager to see what Adam and Emily had created.

The doors swung open on time, and a wave of people started flooding into the building, with their faces alight with wonder and curiosity. Adam and Emily greeted each visitor with warm smiles, welcoming them into the sanctuary centre with open arms.

Inside the waiting area, the space buzzed with energy as people queued to explore the exhibits. There were new interactive displays, and a beautiful diversity of marine and tropical life. The Staff were great showing them around on the tours. The Rescue tanks were incredibly popular with the big fish, and we couldn't wait for the others to join them in the Centre Pool Tank.

The second floor was the exhibition and planted tanks room where it was showcasing what was possible with or without fish in glass tanks. It was also a place of refuge for the troubled minds to plant their problems and watch them change into beautiful bio ecosystems and habitats.

The cafe hummed with activity as patrons sipped coffee and savoured delicious pastries while taking in the breathtaking views of the harbour and mountain.

Throughout the day, Adam and Emily were overwhelmed by the outpouring of support and enthusiasm from the community. Although entrance was free, there was a donation box to help towards running costs and fish food ect. It was a momentous occasion, a celebration of dreams realised and possibilities unleashed, they just did not expect people to be queuing all day. As the sun dipped below the horizon and the day drew to a close, Adam and Emily stood together, watching as the last of the visitors made their way home towards the exits. They knew that their journey was far from over, but in that moment, they allowed themselves to bask in the glow of their achievement, grateful for the opportunity to make a difference in the world.With that in mind, Emily reminded Adam there was a lot of washing up to do in the kitchen.

With hearts full of hope and determination, Adam and Emily looked ahead to tomorrow, ready to chart new waters and continue their journey to protect and preserve the wonders of the ocean for generations to come as this was only the beginning.

Chapter 8: Navigating Challenges

In the days following the grand opening, Adam and Emily faced a new set of challenges as they navigated the realities of running their sanctuary centre. From managing daily operations to ensuring the well-being of the marine life in their care, they encountered obstacles that tested their resolve and ingenuity.

They grappled with issues ranging from equipment malfunctions to delivery delays, but each challenge was met with determination and resourcefulness as always on Emily's part. With the support of their dedicated team and the guidance of their fellow marine biologists, Adam and Emily tackled each problem head-on, finding creative solutions and learning valuable lessons along the way running such a large adventure. One huge aspect is keeping all the pumps going and checking all the temperatures are correct daily but since the new installation of the heating system the worry has been greatly reduced meaning Adam can leave the gallery in the evening knowing it's all safe. Then there's Emily starting to do stock checks for tomorrow just as they are about to leave, so it was at that moment they realised that they had changed so much and laughed it off as they made their way to the car and headed home.

Chapter 9: Making Connections

Despite the challenges they faced, Adam and Emily found joy and fulfilment in the connections they forged with visitors to their sanctuary centre. Each day brought new faces and stories, each one adding to the tapestry of experiences that made their work meaningful. They were touched by the stories of people whose lives had been changed by their experience at the centre, from children who discovered a love for marine biology to adults who found solace and inspiration in the beauty of the ocean.

Children squealed with delight as they peered into the tanks, their eyes widening with wonder at the colourful array of fish and corals. Adam and Emily watched with delight as young minds absorbed the mysteries of the ocean, their curiosity sparking a newfound appreciation for the natural world in all these different tanks.

Adults lingered in front of exhibits, their faces alight with fascination as they learned about the delicate balance of marine ecosystems and the threats facing our oceans. Adam and Emily engaged them in conversation, sharing stories and insights gleaned from years of study and exploration.

But it wasn't just the educational aspects of the sanctuary centre that resonated with visitors—it was the sense of connection and belonging they found within its walls. Families gathered around interactive displays, laughing and learning together. Couples strolled hand in hand through the corridors, lost in conversation as they marvelled at the wonders of the sea.

In every interaction, Adam and Emily saw the transformative power of their small sanctuary centre at work. It was more than just a place to learn about marine life—it was a sanctuary for the soul, a refuge from the stresses of daily life where people could reconnect with the beauty and majesty of the natural world.

As the days turned into weeks and the weeks into months, Adam and Emily's bond with their visitors grew stronger but their desire for bigger and more species keeps Adam up at night but he has to explain this to Emily. In the meantime, they were touched by the stories of people whose lives had been changed by their experience at the sanctuary centre—from children who discovered a love for marine biology to adults who found solace and inspiration in the beauty of the ocean and peace it brought to them without being freezing cold on the shore line.

Through their interactions with visitors, Adam and Emily realised the profound impact their sanctuary centre was having on the community. It had become more than just a place to learn about marine life or fish but it was a place of connection, discovery, and transformation. Adam made many new friends in this interesting world of fish. They never imagined just how popular this hobby was on such a small island but it was clear to see that people wanted to learn and protect their marine environments more than they first thought.

And as they looked ahead to the future, Adam and Emily knew that their journey was far from over. But they also knew that with each passing day, their sanctuary centre would continue to grow and be an inspiration for all who crossed its threshold.

Chapter 10: Looking Ahead

As the months passed, Adam and Emily's sanctuary centre continued to thrive, drawing visitors from near and far and receiving great reviews in the media, with its captivating exhibits and engaging programs it was a huge hit with everyone who came.

With each passing day, their vision for the future grew clearer, somewhere to expand the sealife centre and include other businesses to join in and sublet outlets off the centre. These were just a few of Adam's dreams but they made sense to other businesses so he began to explore new ideas and ways to expand and enhance their offerings as a group of animal enthusiasts to the town on a bigger scale.

They dreamed of creating educational programs for schools, hosting workshops and events for the community, and partnering with other organisations and charities like Wildlife Sanctuary, Dolphin and Whale Watch to further their mission of ocean conservation. Their sanctuary centre had become a beacon of hope and inspiration for the town of Ramsey, and Adam and Emily were determined to build on its success and continue making a positive impact on the world so they asked everyone to spread the word about seaworld.

But even as they looked ahead to new opportunities and challenges, Adam and Emily remained grounded in their commitment to their core values. They knew that the success of their sanctuary centre was not measured in pounds and pennies, but in the hearts and minds of the people it had touched.

As they reflected on the journey that had brought them to this point, Adam and Emily felt a deep sense of gratitude for the support of their community, the dedication of their team, and the beauty of the ocean that had inspired it all. They knew that the road ahead would be filled with twists and turns, but they faced it with hearts full of hope and determination, ready to chart new waters and continue their journey.

All they wanted was their legacy of their work to live on in the hearts and minds of those who had been touched by their sanctuary centre, inspiring future generations to cherish and protect the wonders of the oceans and rivers. Adam and Emily knew that their journey was far from over as they looked ahead to their future dreams of a larger Sealife Centre based on what this sanctuary has already achieved, anythings possible. The couple with hearts full of hope and gratitude for the opportunity to make a difference in the world, went on talking all night releasing their dream but first they had to sell it.

And as they looked out over the horizon, Adam and Emily knew that the best was yet to come.

Chapter 11: Weathering the Winter

As the crisp chill of winter descended upon Ramsey, Adam and Emily found themselves facing a new set of challenges. The winter months were always tough for businesses in the coastal town, with visitor numbers dwindling and operating costs steadily increasing.

Adam and Emily watched with concern as the crowds that had once filled their sanctuary centre during the warmer months grew sparse. The winter weather kept many visitors at home, and those who did venture out used the cafe as a gathering for warmth as most were often deterred by the cold weather.

Meanwhile, the costs of running their sanctuary centre continued to mount. Heating bills soared as they struggled to keep the building warm and comfortable for visitors, while maintenance costs increased as the wear and tear of constant use took its toll on the facility.

Despite these challenges, Adam and Emily refused to lose hope. They knew ways around things and were forever resourceful. The winter months were just a temporary setback, and they remained committed to weathering the storms and emerging stronger on the other side.

They brainstormed creative solutions to attract visitors during the winter months, from hosting special events and workshops to offering discounted admission rates for local residents. The Cafe was turned into a Restaurant dining room in the evening hosting exclusive menus for limited nights. They even reached out to schools and community groups, inviting them to take part in educational programs and field trips designed to showcase the wonders of the ocean even in the coldest of weather.

Slowly but surely, their efforts began to bear fruit. Visitors trickled back to the sanctuary centre, drawn by the promise of warmth, entertainment, and the chance to escape the winter doldrums. Adam and Emily greeted each one with open arms, grateful for their continued support and determined to make their visit a memorable one. Guests were now leaving great reviews again.

As the winter months wore on, Adam and Emily's sanctuary centre emerged from the cold stronger and more resilient than ever before. They had weathered the storm together, proving that even in the darkest of times, the light of hope and perseverance could shine through.

And as the first signs of spring began to appear on the horizon, Adam and Emily knew that brighter days were ahead. With renewed determination and unwavering optimism, they looked forward to the future, ready to face whatever challenges came their way with hearts full of hope and courage.

Chapter 12: Springtime Surprises

As the winter chill began to thaw and signs of spring emerged in Ramsey, Adam and Emily found themselves greeted by a new wave of activity at their sanctuary centre especially after the success with the restaurant reviews.

The changing season brought with it an abundance of life as fish began their annual mating rituals, filling the waters with a flurry of activity and colour once again.

Adam and Emily watched with awe as the tanks in their sanctuary became a stage for nature's spectacle, with fish darting and dancing in a mesmerising display of courtship. It was a reminder of the beauty and wonder of the natural world hidden in our rivers and oceans, and Adam and Emily were determined to capture it on video for all to see on their new channel.

With excitement coursing through their veins, Adam and Emily set to work, setting up breeding more tanks to hold the new species that had appeared in their tanks. They carefully monitored water conditions, temperature, and other factors to ensure the health and well-being of the fish daily, knowing that their success could help to bolster populations and protect other vulnerable species.

But they knew that they couldn't do it alone. In order to properly identify and verify the species they were working with, Adam and Emily reached out to experts at the marine museum in London. They sent samples of the fish for analysis, eagerly awaiting the results that would confirm their suspicions and validate their efforts on any new species.

Weeks passed as Adam and Emily anxiously awaited word from the museum. They busied themselves with preparations for the upcoming breeding season, fine-tuning their systems and protocols to ensure the best possible environments for all their new arrivals.

And then, finally, the long-awaited news arrived. The experts at the marine museum had confirmed the identities of the fish, validating Adam and Emily's work and affirming the importance of their sanctuary centre in the conservation of marine life. They were awarded Best new breeders and new species breeder. Naming the new fish type Emiliadamis River Catfish.

With a sense of pride and satisfaction, Adam and Emily redoubled their efforts, knowing that they were making a difference in the world. As spring unfolded around them, they closely monitor the growth of these freshwater fish and look forward to the new arrivals gracing the larger tanks for everyone to see, each new fish a testament to the power of passion, dedication of the team behind the sea life centre, and also thankful to the wonders of the natural world that we are lucky enough to see it now at this special time in history.

Chapter 13: Welcoming Back the Wonders of the Sea

As the weeks passed and the weather warmed, Adam and Emily noticed a shift in the atmosphere at their sanctuary centre. The arrival of spring had brought with it a renewed sense of energy and excitement, and visitors returned in droves to bask in the beauty of the ocean.

The sanctuary centre buzzed with activity as people of all ages explored the exhibits, interacted with marine life, and immersed themselves in the wonders of the sea. Families ate on the top floor, while children laughed and played in the interactive play areas. Things were going well and steady again.

But it wasn't just the human visitors who were drawn to the sanctuary centre—it was the marine life itself. As the seas warmed, pods of dolphins returned to the waters off the coast of Ramsey, their playful antics delighting visitors and staff alike. Humpback whales breach the surface in spectacular displays of strength and grace, while basking sharks cruise lazily through the shallows off the west coast, their enormous bodies gliding effortlessly through the clear waters.

Adam and Emily watched with awe as the marine life returned to their doorstep, their hearts swelling with gratitude for the beauty and abundance of the ocean once again. It was a reminder of why they had embarked on this journey in the first place—to protect and preserve the wonders of the sea for future generations to enjoy.

As the days stretched into weeks and the weeks into months, Adam and Emily welcomed each new arrival with open arms, knowing that their sanctuary centre was more than just a place to learn about marine life—it was a sanctuary for all who called the ocean home, human or fish.

And as they looked out over the waters of Ramsey, Adam and Emily knew that they were exactly where they were meant to be, surrounded by the beauty and majesty of the ocean and the endless possibilities that lay ahead.

Chapter 14: Embracing the Journey

As Adam and Emily reflected on the past year, they realised that their journey had been a marathon, not a sprint. Building and maintaining their sanctuary centre had been a labour of love, requiring patience, perseverance, and unwavering dedication.

Through the highs and lows, they had learned valuable lessons about the delicate balance of life in the ocean and the importance of protecting and preserving its wonders. They had witnessed firsthand the resilience of marine life and the power of community to effect positive change.

Ramsey had become their home—a place of beauty, inspiration, and endless possibilities. The people of Ramsey had welcomed them with open arms, embracing their vision and supporting them every step of the way. They felt so lucky, so that's why they wanted to always give back where they can.

As Emily watched Adam nurture his tropical worlds and breathe new life into their sanctuary centre, she realised just how important the marine world was to him. It wasn't just a job—it was a passion, a calling, a way of life for them now.

And as they stood together on the shores of Ramsey one sunny afternoon, surrounded by the sights and sounds of the sea, Adam and Emily knew that they were exactly where they were meant to be. They had found their place in the world, and they were determined to protect and preserve it for generations to come. It was at that moment Adam, started running around the beach trying to write in the sand..eventually writing.. Emily.. Will You.. Be My... Forever happy after and ... Marry Me?

She couldn't believe her amazement as she had no idea, none. None whatsoever as Adams never mentioned it and that was the last thing he'd ever want to do after his last relationship so Emily was totally in shock and started crying, whilst trying to answer "yes' ' of course if you'll have me forever.."

The two both bursting with love and pride and with hearts full of hope and gratitude, Adam and Emily embraced the journey that lay ahead, knowing that with each passing day, they were making a difference in the world. And as they looked out over the horizon at that moment, they knew that the best was yet to come and smiled as big as the sunset.

Chapter 15: Answering the Call

On a sunny, warm day in Ramsey, the tranquillity of the coastal town was interrupted by a call to action. The MSPCA received reports from local fishermen about a distressed whale entangled in fishing gear just off the coast. Urgent assistance was needed to rescue the majestic creature, but time was of the essence.

As news of the stranded whale spread across media channels, a call went out for a specialist to assist in the rescue effort. Without hesitation, Emily sprang into action and called them as she was in the north of the island so was quick to respond. With a sense of determination and purpose, she knew that she had to do everything in her power to help save the whale and restore it to its natural habitat so she grabbed her diving gear and equipment waiting for the callback to assist. Within 5 minutes they called back with urgency.

With adrenaline coursing through her veins, Emily rushed to the scene. She joined a team of volunteers, experts, and officials who had assembled to coordinate the rescue operation. Together, they formulated a plan of action on the short boat trip out to the whale and other gathers by now. Only specialist divers are prepared to dive down to the depths to cut free the trapped whale.

As Emily descended into the water, her heart pounded with anticipation. The whale quickly loomed before her, its immense size and strength a stark reminder of the gravity of the situation. Her and another diver wrestled with the ropes and managed to get close enough. With steady hands and unwavering resolve, Emily worked tirelessly to carefully remove the fishing gear that ensnared the creature and weighted it down for however long but the whale was exhausted, all the while mindful of the delicate balance of life in the ocean.

An hour passed as Emily and the rescue team worked tirelessly to free the whale from its entanglement. With each passing moment, the stakes grew higher, but Emily remained focused on the task at hand, determined to see the rescue through to the end as she was getting close but needed to still clear the head which was taking the longest as the whale tired.

Finally, after what felt like an eternity, the last of the fishing gear was removed, and the whale was freed from its captivity with the fishing ropes. With a powerful surge of its tail, the majestic creature swam away into the open sea, a testament to the power of compassion, courage, and cooperation.

As Emily surfaced from the water, exhausted but elated, she knew that she had played a small part in something truly extraordinary. The rescue of the whale was a reminder of the interconnectedness of all life in the ocean and the importance of protecting and preserving its wonders for future generations to enjoy.

And as she looked out over the vast expanse of the sea, Emily felt a sense of peace and fulfilment wash over her. In that moment, she knew that she had answered the call to action with all her heart and soul, and she was grateful for the opportunity to make a difference in the world. As she knew that morning, that whale made a conscious effort to ask for help that day in the bay as it was nearly on its final days so Emily knew it was a special calling for her. She could not wait to tell Adam what she had done and how the whale looked at her at the end with gratitude and soulace.

Chapter 16: A Triumph on the Shore

As Emily emerged from the rescue boat, exhausted yet exhilarated, she was met with a scene of jubilation on the shoreline. The people of Ramsey had gathered in anticipation watching, their eyes fixed on the horizon as they awaited news of the whale's fate.

When Emily finally stepped onto the shore, she was greeted with cheers and applause from the gathered crowd as they were told of its release. Adam rushed forward to envelop her in a tight embrace, his eyes shining with pride and admiration for his brave and compassionate partner in crime, although he wouldn't admit he was scared for her and worried.

Reporters clamoured for Emily's attention, eager to hear her firsthand account of the rescue. But amidst the chaos and excitement, Emily couldn't shake the memory of the moment when she locked eyes with the trapped whale beneath the waves.

In that brief, fleeting moment, Emily felt a connection with the majestic creature unlike anything she had ever experienced before. It was as if the whale had sensed her presence, understood her intentions, and trusted her to set it free.

As Emily recounted her experience to the reporters, her voice trembled with emotion. She spoke of the whale's silent strength and resilience, of the trust it had placed in her to rescue it from its plight. And as she spoke and trembled, she knew that this was a moment she would carry with her for the rest of her life as she turned to Adam.

The buzz on the beach was palpable as people shared their own accounts of the rescue, each one filled with awe and wonder at the sight of the whale breaking free from its bonds. It was a moment of triumph and celebration, a testament to the power of compassion and cooperation in the face of adversity they will always remember.

As the sun dipped below the horizon, casting a golden glow over the gathered crowd, Emily felt a sense of peace and fulfilment wash over her. In that moment, she knew that she had made a difference in the world and in Ramsey, and she was grateful for the opportunity to play a part in something truly extraordinary. She finally felt at home.

Chapter 17: Sharing Stories

As the evening wore on and the adrenaline from the day's events began to fade, Emily found herself opening up to Adam in a way she never had before. Sitting together in the comfort of their home, she recounted her travels to South Africa and Australia, and the harrowing encounter she had with a juvenile great white shark.

Adam listened intently as Emily spoke, his eyes filled with concern and curiosity. He had always admired her adventurous spirit, but he had never realised just how close she had come to danger on her travels.

As Emily described the moment when the shark had attacked, Adam's heart clenched with fear. He couldn't imagine the terror she must have felt in that moment, facing down one of the ocean's most feared predators.

But as Emily continued her story, recounting the efforts of the professional team to distract the shark and keep her safe, Adam felt a swell of pride and admiration for his brave partner. He had always known that Emily was fearless, but now he saw just how courageous she truly was.

When Emily finally revealed the scar on her arm, a memento of her brush with death, Adam's heart ached with sorrow and empathy. He reached out to gently touch the scar, his fingers tracing the faint outline of the wound.

"It must have been terrifying," Adam whispered, his voice filled with emotion. "I'm so grateful you're safe."

Emily nodded, her eyes shining with tears. "It was," she admitted. "But I was lucky. I had a team of professionals looking out for me. Not everyone is so fortunate but it wasn't the sharks fault it was mine as I was in his zone and he was checking me out so when I put my arm out to push his nose away his teeth came down as his jaw went up, there was a lot of teeth as he was a baby really but big enough at 2.5m." Adam couldn't quite believe what he was hearing but he was just amazed at his new Fiance - this little girl, he thought - braver than lions taking on sharks now freeing whales.. "She's amazing, he said, as he couldn't believe who Emily really was and as if she loved him enough to marry him. He always said to follow his heart with this one as this love found him this time.

As the evening drew to a close, Adam held Emily close, his arms a silent promise to protect her from harm. They had shared a moment of vulnerability and intimacy, and Adam felt closer to Emily than ever before, he asked her about the engagement but she reassured him that she just wanted a life with Adam here in Ramsey now like they dreamt of all those moons ago.

And as they drifted off to sleep, wrapped in each other's arms, Adam knew that their love was stronger than ever, new love was stronger than any fear or past darkness, and that together, they could face whatever challenges life threw their way now he'd found his partner in crime. He felt incredibly lucky as they slept.

Chapter 18: The Spotlight

The next day the attention that Emily and Adam's sanctuary centre received in the wake of Emily's heroic rescue of the whale was nothing short of overwhelming. The town of Ramsey buzzed with excitement and pride, it seemed as though everyone was talking about the couple and their incredible efforts to protect marine life and mow saving whales.

News of the whale rescue spread like wildfire, making headlines across the country and even garnering attention from international media outlets. Everyone wanted to interview Emily about the whale but they sheltered at the centre and talked about a plan.

Emily and Adam found themselves thrust into the spotlight, their faces gracing the covers of newspapers and TV reports, their story shared and celebrated by people around the world as videos went viral after drone footage was released showing the boats and divers surrounding the 30ft monster so news teams put the footages together exposing Emily's heroics.

At first, the attention was exhilarating as it was focused on the Whale and then the Sanctuary, just as proud Emily and Adam were of their accomplishments, they embraced the coverage as a validation of their hard work and dedication if it meant more coverage for the sealife centre. They realised the positive impact their sanctuary was having on the world via social media so they thought to top up that presence and include their new whale adventures on their channel, and promote how grateful they were for the opportunity to live there and to raise awareness about the importance of ocean conservation and marine life as this was the perfect storm. This video became a huge hit for them and many inquiries came from it.

But as the spotlight lingered on Emily too long and Adam began to feel the weight of expectations bearing down on them. They were no longer just a couple running a sanctuary centre—they were symbols of hope and inspiration, role models for others to emulate and a couple of local celebrities now after being in the papers and on the tv and now on the social video channels. Emily was gathering a lot more attention especially enquiries for photo shoots with her wet suits which left them thinking a lot as a couple. However Adam was 100% behind her, she said, they could use all this attention ie extra money and put into the fund for SeaWorld. They focused hard on the important things and Adam was behind anything Emily wanted to do so he was happy if she was happy doing her online content again and let those channels grow they thought.

With the increased visibility came scrutiny and criticism, as armchair experts and self-appointed pundits dissected their every move and decision making out they were only to make money and were fake ect. Emily and Adam found themselves constantly second-guessing themselves, worried that they would make a misstep or fall short of the lofty expectations that had been placed upon them. As they searched online they found nothing but only positive news but as the days turned into weeks, the pressure only intensified just in case but they realised they could not live life like this worried about online threats. The fish mattered more.

Emily and Adam longed for the simplicity and quietude of their old lives before the spotlight had found them, but they knew that there was no turning back now.

In the midst of the chaos and uncertainty, Emily and Adam found solace in each other's arms. They leaned on one another for support,

As the islanders celebrated their newfound fame with a glass of wine together, Emily and Adam longed for the simplicity and quietude of their lives before the spotlight had found them. They talked about the days when they could walk down the street without being recognized, when their sanctuary centre was just a dream on the horizon but they soon realised that they don't do boring or quiet things so they say they should have known better. But how would you know if you didn't try and find out, they reminded themselves.

But amidst the chaos and uncertainty, Emily and Adam found strength in the unwavering support of their fellow islanders sending messages of support and help with anything. They leaned on one another for support, drawing courage from the knowledge that they were not alone in their next journey drawing strength from their love and commitment to each other.

And as they navigated the challenges of newfound fame and responsibility, Emily and Adam vowed to stay true to themselves and their island community. They knew that the road ahead would be difficult, but they were determined to weather any storm together, secure in the knowledge that they were making their island proud.

Chapter 19: Facing New Challenges

Despite the outward appearance of success and admiration, behind the scenes, Adam and Emily were facing mounting challenges. The sanctuary was thriving, drawing in visitors and gaining praise from the community, but the reality of running such an operation was beginning to take its toll.

As the number of visitors increased overall, so too did the operating costs. Maintenance, utilities, and staffing expenses were higher than ever before, and Adam found himself struggling to keep up with the financial demands and juggling the sanctuary.

To make matters worse, the recent break-in had left the couple reeling. Adam had tried to shield Emily from the full extent of their financial woes, but the break-in had forced his hand. He couldn't hide the truth any longer so Adam explained one day.

With a heavy heart, Adam sat Emily down and confessed the extent of their financial struggles. The bills were piling up, and despite their best efforts, they were barely scraping by. The recent increase in insurance premiums had only added to their financial burden, and Adam knew that they couldn't keep ignoring the problem. They'll have to start selling some of their collection.

Emily listened in stunned silence as Adam laid bare the challenges they were facing. The break-in had been a wake-up call, a stark reminder of the fragility of their sanctuary centre and the need to confront their financial reality head-on.

Together, Adam and Emily surveyed the damage to the office, the chaos and destruction was a stark contrast to the serenity of the sanctuary centre. But amidst the wreckage, they found a glimmer of hope—a determination to rebuild and persevere in the face of adversity because if they did not then who would.

As they cleaned up the mess and assessed the damage, Adam and Emily made a vow to each other they would not let this setback define them. They would rise above it, stronger and more resilient than before and just move on when asked about it.

And as they looked out over the centre, battered but unbowed, Adam and Emily knew that they were not alone in their struggle. They had the support of their fellow island rescuers, and together with the animals, they would overcome whatever challenges came their way next.

Chapter 20: A Promise Renewed

Standing amidst the all the work to do still, they looked out over the sanctuary centre, their beacon of hope and inspiration amidst the chaos, Adam and Emily knew that they had a responsibility to themselves and to others to persevere. They would be a shining example of resilience and determination, showing the world that no matter what life threw at them, they would rise above it and just get on ad do it as it was only them there left.

And so, with renewed determination and a steadfast commitment to their dreams, Adam and Emily set to work rebuilding their centre and getting it respectable. They knew that the road ahead would be difficult, but they faced it with courage and optimism, secure in the knowledge that they had each other and the unwavering support of their community.

As they laid the foundation for their new found beginning, Adam and Emily promised to never lose sight of their vision—to create and grow a sanctuary for marine life, a place of wonder and inspiration where people could come together to learn, explore, and connect with the natural world. He wanted to bring the sharks on shore and showcase their epic power. They worked all night taking care of the sanctuary and its animals as it was ultimately their favouroirte place to be, with their animals.

And as they watched the first beams of sunlight break through the clouds that morning, casting a warm orange glow over the sanctuary centre, Adam and Emily smiled as they knew that their journey was far from over. It was just beginning so whatever happens next they would be prepared.

THE END

"Charting New Waters" follows the inspiring journey of Adam and Emilys second book, **"Roots of Resilience: Nurturing Change"** as they embark on a new endeavour to establish a sea and fish life sanctuary centre in the coastal town of Ramsey. Driven by their passion for marine conservation and mental health awareness, Adam and Emily navigate the challenges of securing funding and transforming an old building into a sanctuary centre, they face both triumphs and setbacks. From rallying community support to overcoming financial struggles, the couple demonstrates unwavering determination and resilience in the face of adversity.

The narrative unfolds against the backdrop of Ramsey's picturesque coastline, where Adam and Emily's sanctuary centre becomes a beacon of hope and inspiration for both locals and visitors alike. Through heartwarming encounters with marine life and courageous acts of rescue, the couple's dedication to their cause shines brightly, illuminating the path towards a brighter future for both the town and its inhabitants.

"Charting New Waters" follows the inspiring journey of Adam and Emily as they embark on a new endeavour to establish a sea and fish life sanctuary centre in the coastal town of Ramsey. Driven by their passion for marine conservation and mental health awareness.

"Charting New Waters" is a tale of love, passion, and perseverance, highlighting the transformative power of compassion and the importance of preserving our natural world for generations to come. As Adam and Emily's journey unfolds, you are invited to embark on a captivating adventure filled with hope, courage, and the boundless wonders of the sea.

"CHARTING NEW WATERS: Adam and Emily's Journey to the Sea Life Center"

"Charting New Waters: Adam and Emily's Journey to the Sea Life Center"

"Charting New Waters: Adam and Emily's Journey to the Sea Life Center"

"Charting New Waters: Adam and Emily's Journey to the Sea Life Center"

Also by Paul Smith

The Impact Chronicles
Seeds of Change: A Journey to Ramsey
Roots of Resilience: Nurturing Change
Rising Tide: The Rebirth of Ramsey
Seeds of Renewal: Love's Everlasting Bloom
Journey to the Depths: Angels and Demons
Journey to the Sea Life Centre

Watch for more at wix.pbsmith17@wix.com.

About the Author

Paul smith Artist, Aurthor & Designer. Island resident since 1999
Read more at wix.pbsmith17@wix.com.

www.ingramcontent.com/pod-product-compliance
Lightning Source LLC
Chambersburg PA
CBHW061639130726
47996CB00003B/1362